What Was Communism?
A SERIES EDITED BY TARIQ ALI

The theory of Communism as enunciated by Marx and Engels in *The Communist Manifesto* spoke the language of freedom, allied to reason. A freedom from exploitation in conditions that were being created by the dynamic expansion of capitalism so that 'all that is solid melts into air'. The system was creating its own grave-diggers. But capitalism survived. It was the regimes claiming loyalty to the teachings of Marx that collapsed and reinvented themselves. What went wrong?

This series of books explores the practice of twentieth-century Communism. Was the collapse inevitable? What actually happened in different parts of the world? And is there anything from that experience that can or should be rehabilitated? Why have so many heaven-stormers become submissive and gone over to the camp of reaction? With capitalism mired in a deep crisis, these questions become relevant once again. Marx's philosophy began to be regarded as a finely spun web of abstract and lofty arguments, but one that had failed the test of experience. Perhaps, some argued, it would have been better if his followers had remained idle dreamers and refrained from political activity. The Communist system lasted 70 years and failed only once. Capitalism has existed for over half a millennium and failed regularly. Why is one collapse considered the final and the other episodic? These are some of the questions explored in a variety of ways by writers from all over the globe, many living in countries that once considered themselves Communist states.

the cuban drumbeat

castro's worldview:
cuban foreign policy in a hostile world

PIERO GLEIJESES

LONDON NEW YORK CALCUTTA

Seagull Books 2009

© Piero Gleijeses 2009

ISBN-13   978 1 9064 9 737 8

British Library Cataloguing-in-Publication Data
A catalogue record for this book is available
from the British Library

Jacket and book designed by Sunandini Banerjee, Seagull Books
Printed at Rockwel Offset, Calcutta

To Setsuko Ono
and Letterina Gleijeses

Contents

Acknowledgements

Setsuko Ono has stimulated me along my journey with her probing and frank comments, and has inspired me with her intelligence, her courage and her art. One of her paintings graces this book. The paintings that she exhibited at the 2009 Bienal of Havana—'For Our Beautiful Earth: Resistance to Overwhelming Force and Dreams of Peace'—express with exquisite sensitivity her deep longing for a more just world. They challenge me to be relentless in seeking the truth in my chosen field.

In Havana, Jorge Risquet is a forceful critic and a dear friend; even when we disagree, as we do often,

I admire his intelligence and his knowledge and I learn from his criticism. I have benefited enormously from the wisdom and efficiency of Ivys Silva Jomarrón. Gloria León, one of Cuba's most sensitive intellectuals, has helped me understand her country and saved me from countless gaffes and faux pas.

My research in Pretoria, Windhoek and Luanda would have been less rewarding, and much less pleasant, without the generous help of seven good friends: Claudia Uushona, Thenjiwe Mtintso, Paulo Lara, Isabel Martín, Emiliano Manresa, Pedro Ross and Rosa Fonseca.

In Washington, I owe a special debt to Kelley Kornell, the best coordinator that the US foreign policy department at Johns Hopkins School of Advanced International Studies has ever had; to David Fowkes, my brilliant research assistant; and to my friend Isaac Cohen, always bristling with ideas and good advice. Three outstanding research librarians—Linda Carlson, Kathy Pic Barbara Prophet—have acquired for me the mos dish publications. Dean Jessica Einhorn and Associate Dean John Harrington made it possible for me to spend three months in southern Africa at the most opportune moment.

It has been a true pleasure to work with the gracious and creative Naveen Kishore, founder and publisher of Seagull Books, and the very talented Sunandini Banerjee.

Nancy Mitchell is much more than the foremost expert on Carter's foreign policy. I have never met anyone who writes as well as she does or who is a better scholar. I have benefited from her literary skills, her knowledge and her insightful and probing comments. My debt to her is great and grows. I hope that the intellectual collaboration we began many years ago will continue through many more books, hers and mine.

In April 1989, Mikhail Gorbachev visited Cuba. Some of his closest aides had urged him not to go: Fidel Castro was a political dinosaur, they argued; his policy in the Third World was reckless, and Cuba was a source of tension with the US, whom they were courting. Other aides disagreed. In a memo to Gorbachev, accompanying a draft of the speech the General Secretary would give to the Cuban National

Assembly, Georgi Shakhnazarov noted Cuba's very difficult economic situation, and added: 'I have attempted to include warm words about the significance of the Cuban revolution . . . to give moral support to the Cuban government in this moment that is so difficult for them.'[1]

Gorbachev did not consider Castro a relic of the past:

> I had and have a high opinion of this man, of his intellectual and political abilities. He is, without doubt, an outstanding statesman with a unique destiny. . . . In my conversations with Castro, I never had the feeling that this man had exhausted himself, that he, as they say, 'was a spent force', that his world view was cast in cement, that he was unable to absorb new ideas. It was possible to have a constructive dialogue with him, to attain mutual understanding, to count on cooperation.[2]

In Cuba, Gorbachev was a tactful and respectful guest, and the Cubans appreciated that he did not try to lecture them, give them advice or criticize them. At the press conference after the talks, when a journalist asked Castro, 'What advice did the charming Gorbachev give the Cubans?' Castro quipped, 'Gorbachev is charming precisely because he does not tell other countries what to do.'[3]

Gorbachev assured the Cubans of continuing Soviet support. 'Cuba—it is our revolutionary duty, our destiny to help her,' he wrote after leaving the island.[4] His promises rang hollow, however, against the backdrop of the rapidly deteriorating situation in the Soviet Union and in the Soviet Bloc. Seven months later, the Berlin Wall fell, and, throughout Eastern Europe, Communist regimes crumbled.

Castro had told Angolan President José Eduardo dos Santos in late 1988, as detente between Washington and Moscow blossomed:

> We do not know how the United States will interpret peace and detente, whether it will be a peace for all, detente for all, coexistence for all, or whether the North Americans will interpret 'coexistence' as peace with the USSR—peace among the powerful—and war against the small.

> This has yet to be seen. We intend to remain firm, but we are ready to improve relations with the United States if there is an opening.[5]

There was no opening. Over the next two years, as the Soviet Union teetered on the brink of collapse, US officials pressured Gorbachev, who was anxiously seeking US aid, to cut all Soviet aid to Cuba. The collapse of the Soviet Union in December 1991 meant that Cuba was alone, and in desperate economic straits. Washington tightened the embargo, making it as difficult as possible for third countries to trade with Cuba, even if it meant violating their sovereignty. US officials hoped that hunger and despair would force the Cuban people to turn against their government.

The Burden of the Past

Why such hatred? The answer lies, in part, in Castro's betrayal of the special relationship that had existed between the US and Cuba since the early 1800s, when President Thomas Jefferson had longed to annexe the island, then a Spanish colony; he had even proposed a deal with Napoleon who occupied Spain: the US would give France a free hand in South America if France would give it Cuba. Jefferson's successors embraced the belief that Cuba's destiny was to belong to the US. No one understood this better than José Martí, the father of Cuban independence. In 1895, as Cuba's revolt against Spanish rule began, he wrote: 'What I have done, and shall continue to do is to . . . block with our [Cuban] blood . . . the annexation of the peoples of America to the turbulent and brutal North that despises them. . . . I lived in the monster [the United States] and know its entrails—and my sling is that of David.'[6] The next day he was killed on the battlefield.

In 1898, as the Cuban revolt entered its fourth year, the US joined the war against an exhausted Spain, ostensibly to free Cuba. After Spain surrendered, Washington forced the Platt Amendment on the Cubans, which granted the US the right to send troops to the island whenever it deemed necessary and to establish bases on Cuban soil. (Today, the Platt Amendment lives on in the US naval base at Guantánamo Bay.) Cuba became, more than any other Latin American country, 'an American fiefdom'[7]—until 1959. Then Fidel Castro came to power and tweaked the imperial beak of the American eagle.

When Americans look back at that fateful year of 1959—when it all began—they are struck both by their good intentions and by Castro's malevolence. The US had offered the new leader its friendship—only to be rebuffed. Indeed, President Dwight Eisenhower had sought a modus vivendi with Castro—as long as Cuba remained within the US sphere of influence and respected the privileges of the American companies that dominated the island's economy. Castro, however, was not willing to bow to the US. 'He is clearly a strong personality and a born leader of great personal courage and conviction,' US officials noted in April 1959, and, a few months later, a National Intelligence Estimate reported, 'He is inspired by a messianic sense of mission to aid his people.'[8] Even though he did not have a clear blue-print of the Cuba he wanted to create, Castro dreamed of a sweeping revolution that would up-root his country's oppressive socio-economic struc-ture; he dreamed of a Cuba free of the US. Eisenhower was baffled, for he believed, as most Americans still do, that the US had been the Cubans' truest friend, fighting Spain in 1898 to give them independence. 'Here is a country,' he mar-velled, 'that you would believe, on the basis of our history, would be one of our real friends.' As US his-torian Nancy Mitchell has pointed out, 'Our selec-tive recall not only serves a purpose, it also has repercussions. It creates a chasm between us and the Cubans: we share a past, but we have no shared memories.'[9] Ethnocentrism and ignorance have al-ways been the pillars of the City on the Hill.

The US responded to Castro's challenge in the way it always dealt with nuisances in its backyard: with violence. On Eisenhower's orders, the CIA began planning the overthrow of Castro. In April 1961, three months after John Kennedy's inauguration, about 1,300 CIA-trained insurgents stormed a Cuban beach at the Bay of Pigs—only to surrender en masse three days later.

Flush with this victory, Castro tendered an olive branch. On 17 August 1961, Che Guevara told a close Kennedy aide that Cuba wanted to explore a modus vivendi with the US. Kennedy however was not interested. A few months later, on the President's orders, the CIA launched Operation Mongoose, a programme of paramilitary operations, economic warfare and sabotage designed to visit what Kennedy's assistant Arthur Schlesinger has called 'the terrors of the earth'[10] upon Castro.

Relations with Moscow

Castro enjoyed widespread support among the Cuban population, as the CIA acknowledged, but he understood that only strong Soviet backing could protect his fledgling revolution from US wrath. The fate of Guatemalan President Jacobo Arbenz, overthrown by the CIA in 1954, was a bitter reminder of what befell errant presidents in the US backyard. In January 1959, the Soviets knew very little about Castro; for several months, their only contact was through leaders of the Cuban Communist Party visiting Moscow to vouch for the revolutionary credentials of the new government. In October 1959, a KGB official arrived in Havana, establishing the first direct link between the Kremlin and the new Cuban leadership. Soon, the tempo accelerated: in March 1960, Moscow approved a Cuban request for weapons, and diplomatic relations were established on 8 May that same year. Over 1961, the relationship grew close, even ebullient, as Soviet Bloc arms and economic aid arrived. Castro was charismatic; he seemed steadfast; he worked well with the Cuban communists; and he had humiliated the US at the Bay of Pigs. The Soviet Union would transform the island into a socialist showcase in Latin America.

It was the missile crisis that brought the romance to an abrupt end. Thirty years later, in 1992, Kennedy's Defence Secretary, Robert McNamara, finally understood why the Soviets and the Cubans had decided to place missiles in Cuba: 'I want to state quite frankly with hindsight, if I had been a Cuban leader [in the summer of 1962], I think I might have expected a US invasion. . . . And I should say, as well, if I had been a Soviet leader at the time, I might have come to the same conclusion.'[11] Kennedy's reckless policy meant that Castro had legitimate concerns for his country's security. Added to this was the Kremlin's desire to close the 'missile gap', America's well-publicized overwhelming superiority in strategic weapons.

Kennedy learned that there were Soviet missiles in Cuba on 16 October 1962. On 24 October, the US Navy quarantined the island. Four days later, when Nikita Khrushchev agreed to remove the missiles, he did not bother to confer with Castro—'I don't see how you can say that we were consulted in the decision you took,' Castro wrote Khrushchev.[12] The honeymoon was over.

In the wake of the missile crisis, the US continued paramilitary raids and sabotage operations against Cuba, trying to cripple its economy and to assassinate Castro. US officials were no longer confident that they could topple Castro, but they were determined to teach the Latin Americans the lesson that the price of following Cuba's example would be high. 'Cuba was the key to all of Latin America,' the Director of Central Intelligence told Kennedy in 1962. 'If Cuba succeeds, we can expect most of Latin America to fall.'[13]

While Kennedy promoted subversion in Cuba, Castro promoted revolution in Latin America: 'the virus of revolution is not carried in submarines or ships. It is wafted instead on the ethereal waves of ideas. . . . The power of Cuba is the power of its revolutionary ideas, the power of its example.'[14] The CIA agreed: 'The extensive influence of 'Castroism' is not a function of Cuba's power. Castro's shadow looms large because social and economic conditions throughout Latin America invite opposition to ruling authority and encourage agitation for radical change.'[15]

Cuba, however, did not rely just on the power of its example. 'By 1961–62, Cuban support [for revolution] began taking many forms,' a CIA study noted, 'ranging from inspiration and training to such tangibles as financing and communications support as well as some military assistance.' Most significant was military training. US intelligence estimated that, between 1961 and 1964, 'at least' 1,500 to 2,000 Latin Americans received 'either guerrilla warfare training or political indoctrination in Cuba.'[16]

By 1964, the guerrillas in Latin America had suffered a string of setbacks, and Cuban support for them had become a source of discord with the Soviet Union. The Cubans resented Moscow's growing antipathy for armed struggle in Latin America, and the Soviets were unhappy because Castro's support for guerrilla warfare in Latin America complicated their relations with the US and Latin American governments.

Castro was unbending. At a meeting of Communist parties in Moscow in March 1965, Raúl

Castro—Fidel's brother and Minister of Defence—stressed that it was imperative 'to organize a global movement of solidarity with the guerrillas in Venezuela, Colombia, and Guatemala who . . . are fighting heroically for the independence of their countries.'[17] By 1968, however, the guerrillas had been crushed in Bolivia, virtually wiped out in Guatemala and brutally punished in Colombia and Venezuela. These defeats, and Che's death, taught Havana that a few brave men and women could not by themselves ignite armed struggle in Latin America. 'By 1970 Cuban assistance to guerrilla groups . . . had been cut back to very low levels,' US officials concluded.[18]

This removed a major irritant lodged in Cuba's increasingly strained relationship with the Soviet Union. In the mid- and late 1960s, while US policy-makers publicly lambasted Castro as a Soviet puppet, US intelligence analysts quietly pointed to his refusal to accept Soviet advice and his open criticism of the Soviet Union. 'He has no intention of subordinating himself to Soviet discipline and direction, and he has increasingly disagreed with Soviet concepts, strategies and theories,' a 1968 study concluded, reflecting the consensus of the US intelligence community.[19] Castro criticized the Soviet Union as dogmatic and opportunistic, niggardly in its aid to Third World governments and liberation movements and over-eager to seek accommodation with the US. He made no secret of his displeasure with the inadequacy of Moscow's support of North Vietnam, and, in Latin America, he actively pursued policies contrary to Moscow's wishes. 'If they gave us any advice, we'd say that they were interfering in our internal affairs,' Raúl Castro later remarked, 'but we didn't hesitate to express our opinions about their internal affairs.'[20]

To explain why the Soviets put up with 'their recalcitrant Cuban ally', US intelligence reports noted that they were 'inhibited by Castro's intractability'.[21] The Soviets still saw advantages in their relations with Cuba, a 1967 study observed; they were a symbol of Soviet ability to support even 'remote allies' and had a 'nuisance value vis-à-vis the

US'. Above all, the Soviets drew back from the political and psychological cost of a break: 'How could
the Soviets pull out of Cuba and look at the world or
themselves in the morning? It would be a confession
of monumental failure—the first and only Socialist
enterprise in the New World abandoned—and it
would seriously damage Soviet prestige and be
widely interpreted as a victory of sorts for the
United States.'[22]

By the early 1970s, however, reeling from the
twin failures of his revolutionary offensive in Latin
America and his economic policies at home, Castro
softened towards the Kremlin. Cuban criticism of
Soviet policies ceased, and Havana acknowledged
Moscow's primacy within the socialist bloc. At the
same time, Havana's new approach to armed struggle in Latin America—more subtle, more discrimi-
nating—eased relations with the US. In 1974,
Secretary of State Henry Kissinger concluded that
US policy towards Cuba had become counterpro-
ductive. West European and Latin American governments increasingly resented Washington's

heavyhanded pressure to join its crusade against Cuba, and US public opinion, spearheaded by businesses exploring the growing Cuban market, now favoured peaceful coexistence with the island. Kissinger proposed covert negotiations aimed at normalizing relations. In a secret meeting on 9 July 1975, Cuban and US representatives discussed steps that would lead to an improvement of relations and, eventually, full bilateral ties. Four months later, however, Cuban troops landed in Angola, taking Washington, and Moscow, by surprise. The drums were suddenly deafening.

Africa: The Beginnings

I was among those stunned by this sudden outpouring of thousands of soldiers from a small Caribbean island which, in 1975, reminded me more of a tropical Bulgaria, a well-behaved Soviet client, than a fiery revolutionary outpost. 'You can't understand our intervention in Angola without understanding our past,' a Cuban official later told me. He meant that the Cubans who went to Angola were following in the footsteps of those who, over the previous 15 years, had gone to Algeria, Zaire, Congo Brazzaville and Guinea-Bissau.[23] He also meant, very gently, that my mental construction of Cuba as a tropical Bulgaria was, simply, nonsense.

History, geography, culture and language made Latin America the Cubans' natural habitat, the place closest to Castro's and his followers' hearts, the first place where they tried to spread revolution. But Latin America was also where their freedom of movement was most circumscribed. Castro was, as the CIA observed, 'canny enough to keep his risks low' in the US backyard.[24] Hence, fewer than 40 Cubans fought in Latin America in the 1960s, and Cuba exercised extreme caution before sending weapons to Latin American rebels.

In Africa, Cuba incurred fewer risks. Whereas in Latin America, Havana challenged legal govern-ments and flouted international law, in Africa it confronted colonial powers and defended established states. Above all, in Africa, there was much less risk of a head-on collision with the US. US officials barely noted the Cubans in Africa—until 36,000 Cuban soldiers landed in Angola.

Moreover, the Cuban leaders were convinced that their country had a special empathy for and a special role to play in the Third World beyond the confines of Latin America. The Soviets and their East European allies were white and, by Third World standards, rich; the Chinese exhibited the hubris of a great and rising power, and were unable to adapt to African and Latin American culture. By contrast, Cuba was non-white, poor, threatened by a powerful enemy and culturally both Latin American and African. It was, therefore, a unique hybrid: a Socialist country with a Third World sensibility. This mattered, in a world that was dominated, as Castro rightly understood, by the 'conflict between privileged and underprivileged, humanity against imperialism'[25] and where the major fault line was not between socialist and capitalist states but between developed and underdeveloped countries.

THE CUBAN DRUMBEAT ★

If this were a play—*Cuba's African Journey*—the curtain would rise at Casablanca where a Cuban ship, *Bahía de Nipe*, docked in December 1961. It brought weapons for the Algerian rebels fighting against French colonial rule, and it departed with a precious cargo: wounded Algerian fighters and war orphans from refugee camps. A single ship represented the dual thrust of Cuban internationalism: military aid and humanitarian assistance. In May 1963, after Algeria had gained its independence, a 55-person Cuban medical mission arrived in Algiers to establish a programme of free health care for the Algerian people. ('It was like a beggar offering his help, but we knew that the Algerian people needed it even more than we did, and that they deserved it,' explained the Minister of Public Health.[26]) In October 1963, when Algeria was threatened by Morocco, the Cubans rushed a force of 686 men with heavy weapons to the Algerians, jeopardizing a contract Morocco had just signed with Havana to buy Cuban sugar worth \$184 million, a considerable amount of hard currency at a time when the US was trying to cripple Cuba's economy.

Cuba's interest in sub-Saharan Africa quickened in late 1964. This was the moment of the great illusion when the Cubans, and many others, believed that revolution beckoned in Africa. Guerrillas were fighting the Portuguese in Angola, Guinea-Bissau, and Mozambique. In Congo Brazzaville, a new government proclaimed its revolutionary sympathies. Above all, there was Zaire, where armed revolt threatened the corrupt pro-American regime that Eisenhower and Kennedy had laboriously put in place. To save the Zairean regime, the Johnson Administration raised an army of approximately 1,000 white mercenaries in a major covert operation that provoked a wave of revulsion even among African leaders friendly to the US. In December 1964, Che Guevara went on a three-month trip to Africa. Thomas Hughes, Director of the State Department's Bureau of Intelligence and Research (INR), noted that this 'trip was part of an important new Cuban strategy' to spread revolution in Africa: it would win Havana new friends and it would challenge US influence on the continent.[27] Che offered the Zairean rebels 'about 30 instructors and all the weapons we could spare'; they accepted 'with delight'. Che left with 'the joy of having found people ready to fight to the finish. Our next task was to select a group of black Cubans—all volunteers—to join the struggle in Zaire.'[28] From April to July 1965, 120 Cubans, led by Che, entered Zaire. In August, 250 Cubans, under Jorge Risquet, arrived in neighbouring Congo Brazzaville at the request of that country's government, which feared an attack by the CIA's mercenaries; the column would also, if possible, assist Che in Zaire.

But Central Africa was not ready for revolution. By the time the Cubans arrived in Zaire, the mercenaries had broken the resolve of the rebels, leaving Che no choice by November 1965 but to withdraw. In Congo Brazzaville, Risquet's column saved the host government from a military coup and trained the rebels of Agostinho Neto's Popular Movement for the Liberation of Angola (MPLA) before withdrawing in December 1966.

The late 1960s were a period of deepening maturity in Cuba's relationship with Africa. No longer deluded that revolution was around the corner, the Cubans were learning about the continent. In those years, the focus of Havana's attention in Africa was Guinea-Bissau where rebels fighting for independence from Portugal asked for Cuba's assistance. In 1966, Havana sent military instructors and doctors, and they remained until the end of the war in 1974—the longest and most successful Cuban intervention in Africa before the dispatch of troops to Angola in 1975. In the words of Guinea-Bissau's first president:

> We were able to fight and triumph because other countries helped us . . . with weapons, medicine, and supplies . . . But there is one nation that in addition to material, political, and diplomatic support, even sent its children to fight by our side, to shed their blood in our land . . . This great people, this heroic people, we all know that it is the heroic people of Cuba; the Cuba of Fidel Castro.[29]

Not once did US intelligence reports in the
1960s suggest that Cuba was acting in Latin America or Africa at the behest of the Soviet Union. Instead, they consistently stressed that self-defence and
revolutionary fervour were Castro's main motivations. After his repeated offers for the exploring of a
modus vivendi with the US—in 1961, 1963 and
1964—had been rebuffed, Castro had concluded
that the best defence was offence. He would not attack the US directly, which would be suicidal, but assist revolutionary forces in the Third World, thereby
gaining friends and weakening US influence. 'It was
almost a reflex,' Che's second-in-command in Zaire
remarked, 'Cuba defends itself by attacking its aggressor. This was our philosophy. The Yankees were
attacking us from every side, so we had to challenge
them everywhere. We had to divide their forces, so
that they wouldn't be able to descend on us, or any
other country, with all their might.'[30]

But to explain Cuban activism in the 1960s
merely in terms of self-defence would be to distort
reality—a mistake US intelligence analysts did not

make. There was a second motive force, as CIA and INR freely acknowledged: Castro's 'sense of revolutionary mission'.[31] Report after report stressed the same point: Castro was 'a compulsive revolutionary',[32] a man with a 'fanatical devotion to his cause',[33] who was 'inspired by a messianic sense of mission'.[34] He believed that he was 'engaged in a great crusade' to help free the people of the Third World from the misery and the oppression that tormented them.[35]

These, then, were the dual motivations of Cuban activism in the 1960s: self-preservation and revolutionary idealism. They ran along parallel tracks—until Angola.

Angola

When the Portuguese dictatorship collapsed in April 1974, there were three rival independence movements in Angola: Agostinho Neto's MPLA, Holden Roberto's National Front for the Liberation of Angola (FNLA) and Jonas Savimbi's National Union

for the Total Independence of Angola (UNITA).
Although Portugal and the three movements agreed
that a transitional government would rule until independence on 11 November 1975, civil war
erupted in the spring of 1975. That July, Pretoria
and Washington began parallel covert operations in
Angola, first supplying weapons to both FNLA and
UNITA, then sending military instructors. South
Africa and the US were not pursuing identical ends
in Angola, but both agreed that the MPLA had to be
defeated. Pretoria wanted to shore up apartheid at
home and eliminate any threat to its illegal rule over
Namibia, sandwiched between South Africa and
Angola. South African officials were well aware of
the MPLA's implacable hostility to apartheid and of
its commitment to assist the liberation movements
of southern Africa. (By contrast, UNITA and FNLA
had offered Pretoria their friendship.) Although US
officials knew that an MPLA victory would not
threaten American strategic or economic interests,
Kissinger cast the struggle in stark cold war terms:
the freedom-loving FNLA and UNITA would crush

the Soviet-backed MPLA. He believed that success in Angola would provide a cheap boost to US prestige and to his own reputation, pummelled by the fall of South Vietnam a few months earlier.

The first Cuban instructors for the MPLA arrived in Luanda at the end of August, but Soviet aid to the MPLA was very limited—Moscow distrusted Neto and did not want to jeopardize the SALT II arms control negotiations with the US. By September, Washington and Pretoria realized that the MPLA was winning the civil war not because of Cuban aid (no Cubans were yet fighting in Angola) or superior weapons (the rival coalition had a slight edge, thanks to US and South African largesse), but because, as the CIA station chief in Luanda noted, the MPLA was 'more effective, better educated, better trained, and better motivated'.[36]

Washington urged Pretoria, which might have hesitated, to intervene. On 14 October, South African troops invaded Angola, transforming the civil war into an international conflict.

As the South Africans raced toward Luanda, MPLA resistance crumbled; they would have seized the capital had not Castro decided, on 4 November, to respond to the MPLA's appeals for troops. The Cuban forces, despite their initial inferiority in numbers and weapons, halted the South African on-slaught. The official South African historian of the war writes: 'The Cubans rarely surrendered and, quite simply, fought cheerfully until death.'[37] As the South African operation unravelled and credible evidence surfaced in the Western press that Washington and Pretoria had been working together in Angola, the White House drew back. It claimed, loudly, that it had nothing to do with the South Africans, and it condemned their intervention in Angola. Hence the cry of pain of South Africa's Defence Minister, who told the South African parliament:

> I know of only one occasion in recent years when we crossed a border and that was in the case of Angola when we did so with the approval and knowledge of the Americans. But they left

us in the lurch. We are going to retell the story:
the story must be told of how we, with their
knowledge, went in there and operated in Angola with their knowledge, how they encouraged us to act and, when we had nearly reached
the climax, we were ruthlessly left in the lurch.[38]

Betrayed by the Americans, pilloried as aggres-
sors throughout the world and threatened by growing numbers of Cuban soldiers, the South Africans
gave up. On 27 March 1976, the last South African
troops withdrew from Angola.

US officials responded to the humiliating defeat
with outrage and fury. They blasted the Cubans as
Moscow's mercenaries. Perhaps they believed it. In
any case, the image of Castro as Moscow's proxy
was a comforting myth—it simplified international
relations and cast Cuba's extraordinary actions in a
squalid light. In other words, it sidestepped difficult
questions. As former Under Secretary of State
George Ball has written, 'Myths are made to solace
those who find reality distasteful and, if some find
such fantasy comforting, so be it.'[39]

With the passing of time, the evidence that the Cubans sent their troops to Angola 'on their own initiative and without consulting us [the Soviets]', as a Soviet official writes, has become too compelling to deny.[40] Even Kissinger was forced to reconsider: 'At the time we thought he [Castro] was operating as a Soviet surrogate,' he writes in his memoirs. 'We could not imagine that he would act so provocatively so far from home unless he was pressured by Moscow to repay the Soviet Union for its military and economic support. Evidence now available suggests that the opposite was the case.'[41]

What motivated Castro's bold move in Angola? Not Cuba's narrow interests, not realpolitik. Castro's decision challenged Soviet General Secretary Leonid Brezhnev, who opposed the dispatch of Cuban soldiers to Angola, and risked a serious military clash with Pretoria which, urged on by Washington, might have escalated. The Cuban soldiers would have then faced the full South African army without any guarantee of Soviet assistance. Indeed, it took two months for Moscow to begin to help the

Cubans to airlift their troops to Angola. Further-more, the dispatch of Cuban troops jeopardized re-lations with the West at a moment when they were markedly improving: the US was probing a modus vivendi; the Organization of American States had just lifted the sanctions it had imposed in 1964; and West European governments were offering Havana low-interest loans and development aid. Realpolitik required Cuba to rebuff Luanda's appeals. Had he been a client of the Soviet Union, Castro would have held back.

Castro sent troops because of his commitment to what he has called 'the most beautiful cause',[42] the struggle against apartheid. He understood that with the victory of Pretoria, the Washington axis would have tightened the grip of white domination over the people of southern Africa. It was a defining moment. As Kissinger observed later, Castro 'was probably the most genuine revolutionary leader then in power'.[43]

The tidal wave unleashed by the Cuban victory washed over southern Africa. Its psychological impact and the hope it aroused are illustrated by two statements from across the political divide in apartheid South Africa. In February 1976, as the Cuban troops were pushing the South African army towards the Namibian border, a South African military analyst wrote:

> In Angola, Black troops—Cubans and Angolans—have defeated White troops in military exchanges. Whether the bulk of the offensive was by Cubans or Angolans is immaterial in the color-conscious context of this war's battlefield, for the reality is that they won, are winning, and are not White; and that psychological edge, that advantage the White man has enjoyed and exploited over 300 years of colonialism and empire, is slipping away. White elitism has suffered an irreversible blow in Angola, and Whites who have been there know it.[44]

The 'White Giants' had retreated for the first time in recent history, and black Africans celebrated. 'Black Africa is riding the crest of a wave generated by the Cuban success in Angola,' noted *World*, South

Africa's major black newspaper, 'Black Africa is tasting the heady wine of the possibility of realizing the dream of total liberation.'[45] There would have been no heady dream but, rather, the pain of crushing defeat had the Cubans not intervened.

The impact was more than psychological. Cuba's victory marked the real beginning of Namibia's war of independence. This sprawling, underpopulated country had been a German colony before falling under a South African mandate at the close of World War I; in 1971, the International Court of Justice and the UN Security Council had decreed Pretoria's occupation of the country illegal and ordered South Africa to withdraw immediately.

As Pretoria had feared, Agostinho Neto opened his country to the guerrillas of the South West Africa People's Organization (SWAPO) who were fighting for the independence of Namibia. A South African General noted, 'For the first time they obtained what is virtually a prerequisite for successful insurgent campaigning, namely a border that provided safe refuge.'[46]

A Policy Without Equal

The intervention in Angola marked a dramatic shift in Cuban foreign policy—not of motivation or geographical focus but of scale. Before Angola, about 40 Cubans had fought in Latin America and fewer than 1,400 in Africa. From the late 1970s through the late 1980s, more than 1,000 Cuban military advisers were stationed in Nicaragua but, once again, it was to Africa that the bulk of the Cuban soldiers went: tens of thousands remained in Angola and 12,000 went to Ethiopia between December 1977 and March 1978. It was a policy without equal in modern times. During the cold war, extra-continental military interventions were the preserve of the two superpowers, a few West European countries, and Cuba. And West European military interventions in the 30 years between the rise of Castro and the end of the cold war pale in size and daring compared to those of Cuba; even the Soviet Union sent far fewer soldiers beyond its immediate neighbourhood. In this regard, Cuba was second only to the US.

The scale of Cuban humanitarian assistance also increased dramatically. Between 1963 and 1975, approximately 1,000 Cuban aid workers went to several African countries, South Yemen and North Vietnam. By 1991, more than 70,000 had laboured in Africa, Latin America and Asia at no or very little cost to the host country. The number of foreign scholarship students in Cuba also ballooned.

Cuba's internationalism came at a price, though: political, economic and, above all, human. Two thousand four hundred Cubans lost their lives, and more than 400,000 families suffered the pain of separation from their loved ones. As Castro told President dos Santos, 'The major sacrifice is the human cost, you see? It is asking our people to leave their families behind.'[47]

For Castro, writes Leycester Coltman, British Ambassador to Cuba in 1991–94:

> Progress has always been achieved at a price,
> often at the price of suffering and bloodshed
> . . . The Cuban revolution was not the work of

one man or one generation. It was a historical
process, started in the independence struggles
of the nineteenth century. Thousands had died
fighting for it. It was the duty of the present
generation to save the Revolution, however ar-
duous the task. Even in capitalist countries,
many people looked to Cuba as a beacon of
hope . . . Cuba would not disappoint them.[48]

One may agree or disagree with Castro's view
of history but, from 1959, when he entered Havana
in triumph, until today, this sense of mission has
been the keynote of Castro's extraordinary life.

The Horn of Africa

In February 1977—less than two weeks after Jimmy
Carter's inauguration—the military junta that had
overthrown Emperor Haile Selassie in Ethiopia in
1974 turned further to the left, quashing any linger-
ing US hope of retaining influence there. Five
months later, the junta was rocked by Somalia's invasion—encouraged by ambivalent signals from

Washington—of the Ogaden, a region in eastern Ethiopia inhabited by ethnic Somalis. As the military situation deteriorated, the junta leader, Mengistu Haile Mariam, turned to Cuba, which had begun sending military instructors and doctors to Ethiopia in April, and asked for troops.

Castro's reply was negative. A secret Cuban military history notes, 'It did not seem possible that a small country like Cuba could maintain two important military missions in Africa.'[49] In a cable sent on 16 August 1974, Castro told the head of the Cuban military mission in Addis Ababa:

> We absolutely cannot agree to send Cuban military forces to fight in Ethiopia. You must convince Mengistu of this reality. . . . Despite our sympathy for the Ethiopian revolution and our profound indignation at the cowardly and criminal aggression to which it has fallen victim, it is frankly impossible for Cuba to do more in the present circumstances. You cannot imagine how hard it is for us to constantly deny these requests.[50]

However, as the Ethiopians' military situation deteriorated, Havana reconsidered. On 25 November 1977, Castro decided to send troops to Ethiopia to help repel the attackers. Two days later, Brezhnev wrote Castro a warm message expressing 'our complete agreement with your policy. We are pleased that our assessment of events in Ethiopia coincides with yours, and we sincerely thank you for your timely decision to extend internationalist assistance to Socialist Ethiopia.'[51] Over the next three months, 12,000 Cuban soldiers arrived in Ethiopia and helped defeat the Somalis.

The contrast between the Soviet reaction to the dispatch of Cuban troops to Angola in November 1975 and to Ethiopia in November 1977 is stark: in Angola, Cuba acted without even informing the Soviet Union whereas in Ethiopia there was close consultation. As Castro told Neto, 'In Angola we took the initiative, we acted on our own . . . It was a decision full of risks. In Ethiopia, our actions were coordinated from the very beginning with the Soviets.'[52]

Castro did not send troops to Ethiopia to do the Soviets' bidding, but Soviet military and logistical support allowed him to pursue his desired course. Castro had been very impressed by the Ethiopian revolution, and by Mengistu whom he had met in March 1977. He told East German leader Erich Honecker, 'a real revolution is taking place in Ethiopia. In this former feudal empire the land has been given to the peasants. . . . Mengistu strikes me as a quiet, honest and convinced revolutionary leader.'[53] Hundreds of Cuban documents covering the critical period from late 1976 through the spring of 1978 make clear that Castro's feelings were shared by the three top Cuban officials in Addis Ababa: the ambassador, the head of the military mission and the head of intelligence. With hindsight, we know that Mengistu's policies resulted in disaster. But this was not clear in 1977: though the process was undeniably bloody, the Ethiopian junta had decreed a radical agrarian reform and taken unprecedented steps to foster the cultural rights of the non-Amhara population. Even the US government was impressed;

the CIA noted 'the new rulers' efforts to improve the lot of the disadvantaged',[54] and the State Department reported that the government was focusing on 'improving living standards for all' and that 'much has been accomplished'.[55]

Carter administration officials claimed that the Cuban intervention represented a gross violation of detente and unjustifiable interference in African affairs, but it is difficult to follow their reasoning. Mogadishu had violated the most sacred principle of the Organization of African Unity—the respect for borders inherited at the time of independence. Without this principle, there could be no peace in Africa. As the National Security Council specialist on the Horn pointed out, 'The Soviets and Cubans have legality and African sentiment on their side in Ethiopia. They are helping an African country defend its territorial integrity and countering aggression.'[56] The Cubans fought only to repel the Somali invaders; they refused to fight against the insurgencies that beset Ethiopia. They were instrumental in preventing the dismemberment of

Ethiopia at Somalia's hands. In December 2007, the government of Ethiopia, led by men who overthrew Mengistu, inaugurated the Ethiopian and Cuban Friendship Monument in Addis Ababa, constructed as *The Ethiopian Herald* explained, 'to commemorate the 163 Cuban soldiers who lost their lives' during the 1977–78 war with Somalia.[57] The 'Cuban heroes' had died, President Girma Wolde-Giorgis said, to safeguard the sovereignty of Ethiopia and they 'would be remembered in Ethiopia for posterity'.[58]

Southern Africa

The major impact of Cuban internationalism was in southern Africa. The dramatic intervention in Angola began a process that contributed to the independence of Rhodesia and Namibia, and, ultimately, to the end of apartheid. It pitted Cuba against South Africa and the US.

Pretoria intended to reverse the decision of the 1975–76 Angolan war and replace the MPLA government with Jonas Savimbi, the guerrilla chieftain on whom it lavished aid. Savimbi was, a former British Ambassador to Angola writes, 'a monster whose lust for power . . . brought appalling misery to his people',[59] but for Pretoria he had one great virtue: he sought close ties with South Africa. 'We are working with South Africa to shape a common destiny,' he pledged.[60] If Savimbi could be brought to power, Pretoria would not only gain a friend in Luanda but also strengthen its hold over Namibia because Savimbi promised to expel all SWAPO guerrillas from their camps in Angola. As the CIA stated, 'South Africans regard Namibia as a substantial economic asset as well as a buffer',[61] but even more important were the psychological considerations. The 75,000 whites who lived in the former German colony were South African citizens, and whites in South Africa had long considered Namibia part of the national domain. Abandoning Namibia to hostile black rule—few doubted that SWAPO would win free elections—would have demoralized white South Africans and, worse, given hope to South Africa's restive black majority, already emboldened by Cuba's victory over the troops of apartheid in the 1975–76 war. This would have 'significant consequences for South Africa's domestic situation', a US Presidential Review Memorandum noted.[62] To defend apartheid, Pretoria had to destroy SWAPO and bring down the MPLA government. By late 1976, the South Africans began launching raids from their bases in northern Namibia into southern Angola to attack SWAPO and to assist Savimbi.

Cuban troops were Angola's shield against the South Africans. Even the CIA conceded that the Cuban presence was 'necessary to preserve Angolan independence'.[63] Aware of the South Africans' air superiority, enhanced by their modern military airports in northern Namibia, the Cubans pulled their troops from the border and built a defensive line approximately 250 kilometres north of Namibia. If the South Africans wanted to invade the Angolan heartland, they would first have to cross the Cuban line.

Cuba paid a price. The US, which maintained a large army in Western Europe against a theoretical

Soviet threat, demanded that the Cuban troops leave
Angola despite the real South African threat. President Carter was willing to normalize relations with
Havana and lift the embargo if the Cubans buckled.
In December 1977, two US Congressmen hammered
home this message in a long meeting with Castro. But
Castro refused to budge. Angola was threatened by
South Africa, he said, and 'the Cuban mission in Angola was the defense of the country.' The Congressmen insisted: 'President Carter simply wanted a
statement of Cuba's intention to de-escalate.' Castro
replied: 'this could not be done unilaterally . . . The
Angolan government had to decide this, since the
Cubans were not there on their own account. . . . If
the restoration of relations [with the United States]
was presented in the Angolan context, things would
not advance.'[64] This was the constant refrain: Cuba
would not modify its policy in Africa in response to
US threats or blandishments. Castro told two Carter
emissaries a year later:

> We feel it is deeply immoral to use the blockade
> [the US embargo] as a means of pressuring

Cuba. There should be no mistake—we cannot be pressured, impressed, bribed, or bought . . . Perhaps because the US is a great power, it feels it can do what it wants and what is good for it. It seems to be saying that there are two laws, two sets of rules and two kinds of logic, one for the US and one for other countries. Perhaps it is idealistic of me, but I never accepted the universal prerogatives of the US—I never accepted and never will accept the existence of a different law and different rules.

[. . .] I hope history will bear witness to the shame of the United States which for twenty years has not allowed sales of medicines needed to save lives. . . . History will bear witness to your shame.[65]

Ronald Reagan did not offer normalization on any terms. Instead, his administration made threats. 'I want to go after Cuba,' Secretary of State Alexander Haig told Robert McFarlane, Counsellor to the State Department, in 1981. 'Give me a plan for doing it.'[66] Reagan deemed Cuba one of five coun-

tries responsible for 'the growth of terrorism in recent years', and warned: 'These terrorist states
[Cuba, Nicaragua, Iran, Libya and North Korea] are
now engaged in acts of war against the government
and people of the United States. And under international law, any state which is the victim of acts of
war has the right to defend itself.'[67] His words were
echoed by Secretary of State George Shultz who told
The New York Times: 'It is proper for the United States
to strike at military targets in countries supporting
terrorism, even if the target has no direct connection
with a particular terrorist act.'[68] This was no bluster.
The US launched air strikes against Libya in April
1986. Closer to Cuba, it waged undeclared war
against Nicaragua and mined Nicaraguan harbours.
In August 1985, *The New York Times* published a
report Reagan had sent to Congress the previous
May, which asserted that the use of US soldiers
in Nicaragua 'must realistically be recognized as an
eventual option, given our stakes in the region,
if other policy options fail'.[69] The Cubans took
Reagan seriously, and their military advisers in

On his first visit to Cuba in April 1989, Soviet General
Secretary Mikhail Gorbachev is embraced at Havana
International Airport by Fidel Castro. With an unwit-
ting but firm hand, Gorbachev was leading his country
to implosion, paving the way towards a unipolar world
dominated by the United States. In a major speech in
July 1989, Castro stated, 'If tomorrow or any other day
. . . we were to awaken to the news that the Soviet
Union had disintegrated, even in these circum-
stances—which we hope will never happen—Cuba
and the Cuban revolution would continue its struggle
and its resistance.'[70]

Cubans celebrated their victory over a 1,300-man exile force at the Bay of Pigs. The CIA had recruited, trained and armed the exiles, who bristled with confidence. The Cubans, they told their CIA instructors, would not dare fight against a force that was so obviously supported by the United States. Castro's forces, however, fought with grit. On the second day of the invasion, the CIA used American contract pilots to protect the beachhead because the exile pilots 'were either too tired or refused to fly'.[71] The American pilots attacked the Cuban militia with 'napalm . . . as well as bombs and rockets', the Taylor Commission reported.[72]

On the third day, the exiles surrendered en masse.

In October 1963, Fidel Castro, Raúl Castro and Che Guevara met in Oriente, Cuba, where Castro was directing relief operations during Hurricane Flora, to finalize preparations for sending Cuban troops to Algeria to protect it from Moroccan attacks.

Raúl Castro was a frequent visitor to Moscow. American pundits believed that he was the Kremlin's man in Havana, but the CIA knew better. Raúl's admiration of and respect for the Soviet Union did not stop him from standing up to its leaders. The CIA noted in March 1965 that 'Raúl Castro, who led the Cuban delegation to the Moscow meeting [of Communist parties] early this month, . . . caused considerable discord by his intransigent insistence upon the need to send material assistance to North Vietnam.'[73]

One of the last photographs of Che Guevara shows him in Bolivia. The Bolivian insurgency Che led lasted only a few months—from March to October 1967. Che was wounded and captured on October 8. The next day he was murdered on orders of the Bolivian President. The US government said that his fate should be determined by his Bolivian captors, knowing full well that he would be killed. As a senior CIA official pointed out, Che 'would have been hopeless to debrief' because he was such a 'committed and dedicated man'.[74]

Che Guevara believed that only revolution could rescue the people of Latin America from the abject misery in which they were mired and transform their countries from US vassals into independent nations.

The conditions against which Che fought—abject poverty and the obscene gap between rich and poor—still hold sway in Africa and Latin America. Against this tragic backdrop, the memory of Che is a beacon to a great many people. It is the image of a young man, a dreamer and an activist, who renounced honours and comforts and a family he deeply loved to seek the victory of his dream of justice. Forty years after the Bolivian military murdered Che, the government of Bolivia, led by the first Indian president in the history of Latin America, erected this monument to honour his memory.

On 15 March 1976, Fidel Castro and three African presidents visited the grave of Amílcar Cabral, who had led the independence
movement of Guinea-Bissau. On his right is Agostinho Neto of
Angola. To his left are Luís Cabral of Guinea-Bissau and Ahmed
Sékou Touré of Guinea, representing the two countries that sent
troops to fight alongside the Cubans in Angola.

The Ethiopian and Cuban Friendship Monument in
Addis Ababa honours Cuban soldiers who lost their
lives helping defend Ethiopia against a Somali invasion
in 1977–78. The Somalis, who had been encouraged
by ambivalent signals from the Carter administration,
sought to annex a large swathe of Ethiopian territory.
The 'Cuban heroes' had died, President Girma
Wolde-Giorgis said, safeguarding the sovereignty of
Ethiopia. They 'would be remembered in Ethiopia for
posterity'.[75]

The Wall of Names in Pretoria's Memorial Park commemorates those who 'paid the ultimate price' in the struggle for the liberation of South Africa. The names of more than 2,000 Cubans who died in Angola are inscribed on the Wall. Thenjiwe Mtintso, South Africa's ambassador to Cuba, explained: 'The blood of Cuban martyrs runs deep in the soil of Africa and has nourished the tree of freedom of our motherland.'[76]

General Polo Cintra Frías (*left*) was appointed head of the Cuban military mission in Angola in 1983. Intelligent, sarcastic and outspoken, he became the bête noire of his counterpart, General Konstantin Kurochkin, the head of the Soviet military mission in Angola. Soviet complaints notwithstanding, Polo remained in Angola until September 1986 and when the military situation became particularly difficult in late 1987, he was sent back to Angola to lead the Cuban troops against the South African army.

Jorge Risquet (*right*) was Castro's point man for Africa in the 1980s. The Chief of the General Staff of the Cuban Armed Forces told a Soviet General in 1984, 'In my country whenever we discuss strategy, even military strategy, about Angola, Risquet has to be present, because for many years he has been at the center of everything related to Angola.'[77] Risquet, a man of brilliance and wit, became the bête noire of the Americans in the 1988 negotiations about Angola and Namibia. 'Risquet was difficult,' the head of the US negotiating team, Assistant Secretary for Africa Chester Crocker, told me.[78] He defended the Cuban position with skill and grit. Risquet has written widely, with verve, insight and authority, about Havana's policy in Africa.

Almost 30,000 Africans, Latin Americans and Asians have attended secondary school on Cuba's Island of Youth, with all expenses paid by the Cuban government. Many of the students continued their studies at Cuban universities and technical institutes.

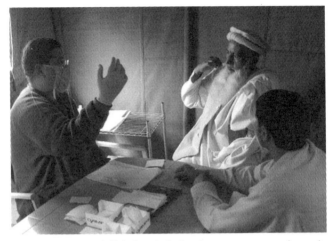

(*Above, and facing page*) Cuba's technical assistance programme began in 1963 and continues to the present day. More than 350,000 Cuban aid workers have served in Latin America, Africa and Asia. For very poor countries the aid has always been free.

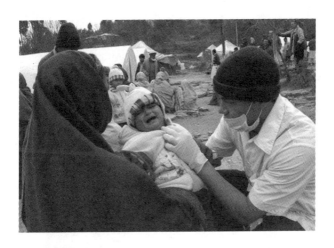

Nicaragua were under orders from Havana to fight if the US attacked. The Americans might retaliate by launching surgical air strikes against Cuba or by imposing a blockade.

The Cubans knew that they would be on their own; Moscow would not help them. They had understood this after the 1962 Missile Crisis, when the Soviets had negotiated over their heads with the US. Castro told a high-level East German delegation in 1968, 'The Soviet Union has given us weapons. We are and will forever be thankful . . . but if the imperialists attack Cuba, we can count only on ourselves.'[79] This had not mattered so much in the 1970s, when the danger of a US attack had receded. But the election of Ronald Reagan changed everything.

To appreciate Cuba's policy in Angola, one must keep in mind this double constraint: the threat from the US, and the fragility of the Soviet shield. In 1986, Castro told Angola's President dos Santos that Cuba had felt—

> . . . constantly under threat, but we hadn't retreated, . . . we had kept helping Angola . . .

How beautiful [*bonito*] this is . . . it is perhaps our most important accomplishment, compañero José Eduardo, that we were threatened . . . and yet we not only refused to withdraw, but we reinforced our troops in Angola . . . I believe that in the history of our revolution, compañero José Eduardo, our internationalist actions are our most important accomplishments, because any other country, seeing itself threatened, would have brought its troops and weapons back to defend the homeland, but we did exactly the opposite—because we had confidence in our people's, in our country's ability to defend itself.[80]

US intelligence was well aware of Cuba's ability to defend itself, and the CIA warned that 'any invasion of Cuba would involve massive American military casualties.'[81]

The Reagan administration saw in South Africa a valuable ally in its struggle to force the Cubans out of Angola. South African Foreign Minister Pik Botha told his colleagues: 'I believe that in the entire period since the Second World War, there has never been a US government as well disposed towards us as the present government.'[82] Reagan's goodwill emboldened the South Africans. From 1981 to 1987, they launched bruising invasions of Angola south of the Cuban defensive line although they never attacked or breached the line itself. They also intensified their aid to Savimbi. The CIA explained in February 1985, 'We believe most key officials in the South African government are determined that Savimbi eventually will take power in Luanda. Savimbi's triumph would at the same time eliminate one of the regimes most hostile to Pretoria in the region and serve as part of a ring of "moderate" buffer states surrounding Namibia.' The South Africans, the CIA predicted, would scuttle any settlement with Angola that did not pave the way for Savimbi's takeover.[83] And they remained, in the words of the US Ambassador to Pretoria, 'implacably' opposed to Namibian independence.[84]

In early 1986, the Reagan administration, with the support of the US Congress, openly engaged in a substantial programme of military aid to Savimbi. Savimbi's human rights record was appalling. Yet as House Foreign Affairs Committee senior staffer Stephen Weissman remarked when trying to explain the motivation behind US policy, 'Savimbi had one redeeming quality: he killed Cubans.'[85]

In September 1987, the South African Defense Force (SADF) unleashed a major attack against the Angolan army in southeastern Angola. By early November, it had cornered the best Angolan units in the small town of Cuito Cuanavale. The UN Security Council demanded that South Africa unconditionally withdraw all its troops from Angola. Publicly, the US joined in the unanimous vote; privately, the Assistant Secretary of State for Africa, Chester Crocker, reassured the South African Ambassador to the US that 'the SAG [South African Government] should take note that the resolution did not contain a call for comprehensive sanctions and did not provide for any assistance to Angola. That was no accident, but a consequence of our own efforts to keep the resolution within bounds.'[86] This gave Pretoria time to annihilate the elite units of the Angolan army. By mid-January, South African military sources and Western diplomats were announcing that the fall of Cuito was imminent.

But Cuito did not fall. Castro sent his best troops and his most sophisticated weapons to Angola, stripping Cuba's defences at home down to the bone. The Iran-Contra scandal of late 1986 had weakened Reagan, and the danger of a US military attack against Cuba, which had haunted the Cuban leaders for six years, had receded. 'For us the greater danger is . . . in Angola,' Castro explained. 'The war is there, not here.'[87]

Once again, as in 1975, the Cubans acted without consulting Moscow. Castro was well aware that Gorbachev was focused on improving relations with the US and was therefore wary of military escalation in southern Africa. 'The news of Cuba's decision to send additional troops to Angola was for us, I say it bluntly, a real surprise,' Gorbachev complained to Castro. 'I find it hard to understand how such decision could be taken without us.'[88] However, as in 1975, the Soviets' irritation gave way to acceptance of the fait accompli, and Moscow supplied many of the additional weapons that the Cubans wanted for their troops in Angola.

Castro wanted to force the SADF out of Angola, once and for all. He would first break the South African onslaught against Cuito Cuanavale in the southeast, then attack in another direction—towards the southwest—'like a boxer who with his left hand blocks the blow and with his right—strikes'.[89]

On 23 March 1988, the SADF launched its last major attack against Cuito, which was, according to a South African officer, 'brought to a grinding and definite halt'. The US Joint Chiefs of Staff noted, 'The war in Angola has taken a dramatic and, as far as the SADF is concerned, an undesirable turn.'[90]

The Cuban left hand had blocked the blow and the right hand was preparing to strike: in the southwest, powerful Cuban columns were moving towards the Namibian border, pushing the South Africans back. Cuban MIG-23s began to fly over northern Namibia.

As a child, in Italy, I heard my father talk about the hope he and his friends felt in December 1941 as they had listened to the radio reports of the German troops leaving the city of Rostov on the Don. It was the first time in two years of war that the German superman had been forced to retreat. I remembered his words—and the profound sense of relief they conveyed—as I read the South African and Namibian press from these months in early 1988. For the blacks of Namibia and of South Africa, the advance of the Cuban columns towards the border, pushing back the troops of apartheid, was a clarion call of hope.

While Castro's soldiers advanced towards the Namibian border, Cubans, Angolans, South Africans and Americans sparred across the table; the Soviets sat on the sidelines. It was Castro who 'was driving the Communist train in Angola,' writes Assistant Secretary Crocker, who led the US team.[91] 'And he did so brilliantly,' Crocker's Senior Deputy

THE CUBAN DRUMBEAT ★

adds. 'It was a model case of the use of force for a diplomatic objective.'[92]

The Cubans' growing military superiority on the ground shaped the negotiations. US and South African officials feared that the Cuban troops would cross the border into Namibia. The US Joint Chiefs of Staff warned that, if the negotiations deadlocked, 'Cuban forces will be in position to launch a well-supported offensive into Namibia.'[93] Crocker sought in vain to determine Havana's intentions. He asked Jorge Risquet, Castro's point man on Africa, but all Risquet would say was: 'the only way to guarantee [that our troops stop at the border] is to reach an agreement [on the independence of Namibia].'[94] A frustrated Crocker cabled Secretary Shultz, 'Reading the Cubans is yet another art form. They are prepared for both war and peace. . . . We witness considerable tactical finesse and genuinely creative moves at the table. This occurs against the backdrop of Castro's grandiose bluster and his army's un-precedented projection of power on the ground.'[95] The South Africans' dilemma was summed up by a close aide of Foreign Minister Pik Botha: if Pretoria continued to oppose Namibian independence, it ran 'the very real risk of becoming involved in a full-scale conventional war with the Cubans, the results of which are potentially disastrous'.[96] The SADF was grim: 'We must do our utmost to avert a confrontation.'[97]

South Africa gave up. In December 1988, in New York, it agreed to UN supervised elections in Namibia and pledged to end all aid to Savimbi, in exchange for a gradual withdrawal of the Cuban troops from Angola spread over 27 months. In March 1990, SWAPO's leader, Sam Nujoma, became the first president of a free Namibia.

There would have been no New York agreements without the Cubans' prowess on the battlefield and skill at the negotiating table. Pretoria's capitulation reverberated beyond Namibia and Angola. As Nelson Mandela said, the Cuban victory 'destroyed the myth of the invincibility of the white oppressor . . . [and] inspired the fighting masses of South Africa . . . Cuito Cuanavale was the turning

point for the liberation of our continent—and of my
people—from the scourge of apartheid.'[98]

Humanitarian Assistance

Castro's battalions in the Third World also included
aid workers, and their ranks swelled after 1975.
Cuban primary-school teachers went to the
Nicaraguan countryside where they taught in im-
provised classrooms and slept in peasants' hovels.
Cuban doctors went to Tindhouf, in southwestern
Algeria, to care for tens of thousands of refugees
from Western Sahara, occupied by Moroccan
troops. Other Cuban doctors created and staffed
medical faculties in Aden, Guinea-Bissau and Jimma
(Ethiopia). The CIA reported: 'The Cuban techni-
cians are primarily involved in rural development
and educational and public health projects—areas
in which Cuba has accumulated expertise and has
experienced success at home.'[99] Doctors, teachers
and construction workers were the flagbearers of
Cuba's humanitarian assistance.

The Carter administration did not object to the presence of Cuban aid workers, but the Reagan administration did. 'They engage in all sorts of activity that we don't welcome,' Kenneth Skoug, the Director of the State Department's Office of Cuban Affairs, explained. 'Sometimes they go into a country and teach people to read. Yet at the same time the things people are learning to read contain political indoctrination. Their engineers build roads, but at the same time the roads are militarily significant.'[100] (Skoug did not mention doctors, but probably they too were subversive—by saving lives, they gained friends for Cuba.)

The largest aid mission was in Angola. 'The abysmal lack of basic skills within the Angolan population'[101] struck every observer: the exodus of 90 per cent of the 320,000 Portuguese living in Angola in 1974 had deprived the country of its skilled labour force, from managers to taxi drivers. Four days after arriving in Luanda in 1976, Raúl Castro informed Havana that 'everyone, from President Neto . . . down to the ordinary people in the most re-

mote corners of the country, is hoping for Cuban assistance. This is natural, given our participation in
the war, the fact that our languages are so similar,
our ethnic background, and the prestige of our revolution.'[102]

The aid had already begun to flow. The first
Cuban doctors arrived in Angola in late November
1975, a few days after the first troops. By late 1977,
there were 3,350 Cuban aid workers, including 223
doctors. Cuba was paying their salaries. When in
March 1984 President dos Santos visited Havana,
he asked Castro, 'How long can Cuba bear this bur-
den?' Castro replied, 'I believe . . . taking into account the situation of Angola, that you must not
worry about this. We can bear it for as long as necessary. Don't worry. We will make this sacrifice.'[103]

The aid workers were volunteers. Some were
doubtless motivated by the desire to impress their
neighbours or the government. Curiosity, and a
sense of adventure, may have influenced many. But
there was much more. These Cubans represented,
according to the CIA, the new generation who had

grown up under Castro, 'instilled with a high degree of nationalism, motivation and self-esteem'.[104] Internationalism—the duty to help others—was at the core of the Cuban revolution. For Castro's followers, and they were legion, this was not rhetoric—'There are no words to express all that I felt, while they bestowed the medal on us,' a young Cuban paediatrician wrote her mother from Angola, after she and four other members of her medical brigade received the Medal of the Internationalist Worker in a simple ceremony, attended by the staff of the hospital where she worked:

> It has been a great day [. . .] full of emotions and of a truth I will never forget: this medal . . . represents the happy culmination of this time, when I've offered my labor to these people who need so much. I will return to my country having fulfilled my duty. Regardless of the bad moments we've faced here, the difficulties and hardships, I feel proud of it all [. . .] and the best that one takes away from here are the moral rewards that transcend anything material.[105]

While Cuban aid workers went abroad, more than 40,000 Africans, Latin Americans and Asians studied in Cuba on full scholarships funded by the Cuban government. 'Among us there are neurologists, gynaecologists, internists, psychologists, dentists, veterinarians, biologists,' an Ethiopian, Berhanu Dibaba, who studied medicine at the University of Havana, said, smiling. 'It has been a good harvest.'[106] In 1996, in French-speaking Conakry, I accompanied a Cuban friend to the Ministry of Agriculture where many spoke to him in Spanish. He laughed at my surprise—all were graduates of Cuban universities, he explained.

The Balance Sheet

Cuban actions in Latin America and Africa in the 1960s—small-scale operations involving a limited number of people—were conducted without direct Soviet assistance, as was the dispatch of the Cuban troops to Angola in 1975 and again in 1987, but none of this would have been possible without the military and economic aid that Moscow gave the island. That is, Cuba's ability to act independently was made possible by the existence of a friendly superpower on which it depended for its economic and military lifeline. This somewhat paradoxical situation parallels the relationship between the US and Israel: it is US military and economic support that makes possible Israel's freedom of manoeuvre. While Havana and Tel Aviv have pursued opposite foreign policies, they do have this one thing in common: dependence on one superpower did not translate into being a 'client'.

Any fair assessment of Castro's foreign policy must recognize its impressive successes, and particularly its role in changing the course of southern African history in defiance of Washington's best efforts to stop it. There is no other instance in modern history in which a small underdeveloped country has changed the course of events in a distant region—humiliating one superpower and repeatedly defying another. There is no other instance in which an underdeveloped country has embarked on a programme of technical assistance of such scope and generosity.

The cold war framed three decades of Castro's revolutionary zeal, but Castro's vision was always larger than it. For him, the battle against imperialism —his life's *raison d'être*—is more than the struggle against the US: it is the war against despair and oppression in the Third World. In July 1991, Nelson Mandela visited Havana and voiced the epitaph to the story of Cuba's aid to Africa during the cold war. His words set off 'a gusher' of criticism in the US. 'We come here with a sense of the great debt that is owed the people of Cuba,' Mandela said. 'What other country can point to a record of greater selflessness than Cuba has displayed in its relations to Africa?'[107]

By then, Cuba stood alone. Its East European allies were gone and the Soviet Union was on the verge of collapse. Many assumed Cuba would be next. I remember listening, in May 1991, to prominent French intellectual, François Heisbourg, as he asserted that, like Nikolae Ceauçescu of Romania, Fidel Castro too was doomed.

Others, less arrogant, less ignorant, understood that Cuba was not Romania, and that Castro still enjoyed widespread support among the Cuban population. They believed that the Cuban revolutionary regime would not only survive in a unipolar world dominated by the US, but also that the demise of the Soviet Union would mean the end of the unique foreign policy that Castro had conducted over three decades, often against the wishes of the Soviet Union, often with its support but never at its behest.

By 1991, Cuba's soldiers and aid workers had returned home. The Cuban government pledged that all foreign students in Cuba would be allowed to finish their studies but no new students would be accepted. In 1994, I attended the graduation ceremony of a group of foreign students. They would be, I believed, among the last.

I was wrong. At the *Escuela Latinoamericana de Medicina*, a few miles west of Havana, thousands of underprivileged youths from Latin America and Africa are studying, all expenses paid, to become doctors—a different breed of doctors, Cuba hopes, with a social conscience that will inspire them to return to their countries to take care of the poor in the rural areas and urban slums. And tens of thousands of Cuban aid workers have returned to the Third World. For very poor countries the aid is still free; the others pay a modest amount. Castro's soldiers have returned home, but Cuba's unique foreign policy—its war against despair and oppression in the Third World—continues.

In Washington, the war against Cuba also continues. As Leycester Coltman, former British Ambassador to Cuba, has written, Fidel Castro is 'still a bone . . . stuck in American throats. He had defied and mocked the world's only superpower, and would not be forgiven.'[108] US officials and pundits ponder what conditions to demand of the errant Cubans before Washington lifts its embargo, forgetting that it is the US that tried to assassinate Castro, carried out terrorist actions against Cuba and continues to occupy Cuban territory—Guantánamo, the filthy lucre of 1898. Their 'selective recall'—so critical to the maintenance of the myth of the City on the Hill—allows them to transform Cuba into the aggressor and the US into the victim. It is not love of democracy or concern for the welfare of the Cuban people that motivates the Americans. The desire for revenge, nothing more, explains US policy towards Castro's Cuba.

Fidel Castro and Nelson Mandela. Painting by Setsuko Ono.

In 1995 Nelson Mandela said, 'Cubans came to our region as doctors, teachers, soldiers, agricultural experts, but never as colonizers. They have shared the same trenches with us in the struggle against colonialism, underdevelopment, and Apartheid. Hundreds of Cubans have given their lives, literally, in a struggle that was, first and foremost, not theirs but ours. As Southern Africans we salute them. We vow never to forget this unparalleled example of selfless internationalism.'[109]

Notes

1   Georgi Shakhnazarov, *Tsena Svobody: Reformatsiya
    Gorbacheva glazami ego pomoshchnika* [The Price of
    Freedom: Gorbachev's Reforms Through His
    Assistant's Eyes] (Moscow: Rossika Zevs, 1993), p.
    384.

2   Mikhail Gorbachev, *Zhizn' i reformy* [Life and Re-
    forms] (Moscow: Novosti, 1995), VOL. 2, p. 425.

3   Castro, quoted in memcon, Hermann Axen,
    Jorge Risquet (Berlin, 14 April 1989). DY30 IVA
    2/20/205, Stiftung Archiv der Parteien und
    Massenorganisationen der DDR im Bunde-
    sarchiv, Berlin (SAPMO).

4   Mikhail Gorbachev, 'Ob itogakh vizita Gor-
    bacheva na Kube' [Results of Gorbachev's Visit
    to Cuba] (13 April 1989). National Security
    Archive, Washington DC (NSA).

5   Memcon, Fidel Castro, José Eduardo dos Santos
    (Havana, 17 December 1988), p. 28. Consejo de
    Estado, Havana.

6   José Martí to Manuel Mercado (18 May 1895), in
    José Martí, *Epistolario* [Letters] (Havana: Centro
    de Estudios Martianos, 1993), VOL. 5, p. 250.

7   Tad Szulc, *Fidel: A Critical Portrait* (New York:
    William Morrow, 1986), p. 13.

8 'Unofficial Visit of Prime Minister Castro of
   Cuba to Washington—A Tentative Evaluation',
   enclosed in Christian Herter to Dwight D. Eisenhower (23 April 1959), *Foreign Relations of the United
   States 1958–60* (Washington DC: United States
   Government Printing Office, 1991), VOL. 6, p.
   483; Special National Intelligence Estimate (NIE),
   'The Situation in the Caribbean through 1959'
   (30 June 1959). NSA.

9 Eisenhower press conference (28 October 1959),
   in US General Services Administration, *Public
   Papers of the Presidents of the United States: Dwight D.
   Eisenhower, 1959* (Washington DC: United States
   Government Printing Office, 1960), p. 271;
   Nancy Mitchell, 'Remember the Myth', *News and
   Observer* (Raleigh, 1 November 1998), p. G5.

10 Arthur Schlesinger, *Robert Kennedy and His Times*,
   (New York: Houghton Mifflin, 1979), p. 516.

11 Robert McNamara, in Laurence Chang and Peter
   Kornbluh (eds), *The Cuban Missile Crisis, 1962: A
   National Security Archive Documents Reader* (New York:
   New Press, 1992), pp. xi–xii.

12 Fidel Castro to Nikita Khrushchev (31 October
   1962), in James Blight, Bruce Allyn and David
   Welch, *Cuba on the Brink: Castro, the Missile Crisis and*

the Soviet Collapse (New York: Pantheon, 1993), p. 491.

13 John McCone, Memo of meeting with President (23 August 1962), in *Foreign Relations of the United States 1961–63* (Washington DC: United States Government Printing Office, 1964), VOL. 10, p. 955.

14 Fidel Castro speech, *Revolución* (Havana, 23 February 1963), p. 4.

15 NIE, 'Latin American Reactions to Developments in and with Respect to Cuba' (18 July 1961). National Security Files (NSF), BOX 8/9, Lyndon B. Johnson Library, Austin, Texas (LBJL).

16 CIA, Directorate of Intelligence, 'Cuban Subversive Activities in Latin America, 1959–1968' (16 February 1968). National Security File Country File (NSFCF), BOX 19, LBJL.

17 'Discurso pronunciado en la reunión consultiva de los Partidos Comunistas y Obreros que se celebra en Moscú' [Speech delivered in the consultative meeting of the Communist and Workers' Parties in Moscow] (3 March 1965). Archives of the Central Committee of the Communist Party of Cuba (ACC).

18 US Department of State, 'Cuban Presence in Africa' (28 December 1977). Freedom of Information Act (FOIA).

19 'National Policy Paper—Cuba: United States Policy' (draft) (15 July 1968). FOIA.

20 Memcon, Raúl Castro, Mengistu Haile Mariam (Addis Ababa, 7 January 1978). ACC.

21 Thomas Hughes to SecState, 'Soviet Intentions toward Cuba' (12 March 1965). NSFCF, BOX 33/37, LBJL.

22 CIA, Board of National Estimates, 'Bolsheviks and Heroes: The USSR and Cuba' (21 November 1967). FOIA.

23 I refer to the former French colony as Congo Brazzaville and the former Belgian colony as Zaire.

24 Special NIE, 'Cuba: Castro's Problems and Prospects over the Next Year or Two' (27 June 1968). NSF, NIE, BOX 8/9, LBJL.

25 'National Policy Paper—Cuba: United States Policy' (draft) (15 July 1968). FOIA.

26 José Ramón Machado Ventura, note to author, 12 July 1995, Havana.

27 Hughes to SecState, 'Che Guevara's African Venture' (19 April 1965). NSFCF, BOX 20, LBJL.

28 Che Guevara, 'Pasajes de la guerra revolucionaria (Congo)' [Moments of the Revolutionary War] (Dar-es-Salaam, December 1965). Havana: private collection, pp. 13–14.

29 Luís Cabral speech, *Nõ Pintcha* (Bissau, 22 January 1977), p. 4.

30 Interview with Víctor Dreke, 11 July 1994, Havana.

31 Denney to SecState, 'Cuban Foreign Policy' (15 September 1967). POL. 1 Cuba, Subject—Numeric Files: 1963–73, Record Group 59, National Archives, College Park, Maryland (NA).

32 Special NIE, 'Cuba: Castro's Problems and Prospects over the Next Year or Two' (27 June 1968). NSF, NIE, BOX 8/9, LBJL.

33 CIA, Directorate of Intelligence, 'Cuban Subversive Policy and the Bolivian Guerrilla Episode' (May 1968). NSFCF, BOX 19, LBJL.

34 Special NIE, 'The Situation in the Caribbean through 1959' (30 June 1959). NSA.

35 NIE, 'The Situation in Cuba' (14 June 1960). NSA.

36 Robert Hultslander (CIA Station Chief, Luanda, 1975), fax to author, 22 December 1998.

37 F. J. du Toit Spies, *Operasie Savannah. Angola 1975–1976* [Operation Savannah. Angola 1975–1976] (Pretoria: S. A. Weermag, 1989), p. 108.

38 P. W. Botha (17 April 1978), Republic of South Africa, *House of Assembly Debates*. Pretoria, COL. 4852.

39 George Ball, *The Past Has Another Pattern: Memoirs* (New York: W. W. Norton, 1982), p. 374.

40 Anatoly Dobrynin, *In Confidence: Moscow's Ambassador to America's Six Cold War Presidents* (New York: Crown, 1995), p. 362.

41 Henry Kissinger, *Years of Renewal* (New York: Simon and Schuster, 1999), p. 816.

42 Fidel Castro, in 'Indicaciones concretas del Comandante en Jefe que guiarán la actuación de la delegación cubana a las conversaciones en Luanda y las negociaciones en Londres (23-4-88)' [Specific Instructions from the Commander-in-Chief to Guide the Cuban Delegation in the Conversations in Luanda and in the Negotitations in London (23-4-88)]. Centro de Información de las Fuerzas Armadas Revolucionarias, Havana (CIFAR).

43 Kissinger, *Years*, p. 785.

44 Roger Sargent, *Rand Daily Mail* (Johannesburg, 17 February 1976), p. 10.

45 'Editorial', *World* (Johannesburg, 24 February 1976), p. 4.

46 Jannie Geldenhuys, *Dié wat gewen het: Feite en Fabels van die bosoorlog* [Those Who Have Won: Facts and Fables from the Bush War] (Pretoria: Litera Publikasies, 2007), p. 45.

47 Memcon, Fidel Castro, José Eduardo dos Santos (Havana, 19 March 1984). CIFAR.

48 Leycester Coltman, *The Real Fidel Castro* (New Haven: Yale University Press, 2003), p. 280.

49 Ministerio de las Fuerzas Armadas Revolucionarias, 'Las misiones internacionalistas desarrolladas por las FAR en defensa de la independencia y la soberanía de los pueblos' [The Internationalist Missions carried out by the Revolutionary Armed Forces in Defence of the Independence and the Sovereignty of the People] (n.d.). CIFAR.

50 Fidel Castro to Arnaldo Ochoa (16 August 1977). CIFAR.

51 Leonid Brezhnev to Fidel Castro (27 November 1977). CIFAR.

52 Memcon, Fidel Castro, Agostinho Neto (Havana, 24 January 1979). Consejo de Estado, Havana.

53 Memcon, Fidel Castro, Erich Honecker (Berlin, 3 April 1977). DY30 JIV 2/201/1292, SAPMO.

54 CIA, Weekly Summary (28 May 1976). CREST, NA.

55 US Department of State, 'Current Foreign Assistance' and 'The Case for Continued Assistance' enclosed in Peter Tarnoff to Zbigniew Brzezinski (May 1978). Warren Christopher Papers, BOX 16, NA.

56 Paul Henze to Zbigniew Brzezinski (1 March 1978). Brzezinski Collection, National Security Assistant, Staff Material, Horn, BOX 1, Jimmy Carter Library, Atlanta (JCL).

57 *The Ethiopian Herald* (Addis Ababa, 18 December 2007), p. 1.

58 *The Ethiopian Herald* (Addis Ababa, 19 December 2007), p. 1.

59 Marrack Goulding, *Peacemonger* (London: John Murray, 2002), p. 193.

60 'Points made by Dr. Jonas Savimbi during a meeting on May 28, 1983'. Samesprekings met Angola, VOL. 2, Department of Foreign Affairs, Pretoria (DFA).

61 CIA, Intelligence Memorandum, 'South Africa's Policy toward Namibia: A Review of Basic Factors' (20 May 1977). RAC, JCL.

62 'Presidential Review Memorandum: Rhodesia, Namibia and South Africa' (early 1977). FOIA.

63 CIA, 'Angola Cuba: Some Strains but No New Developments' (9 April 1979). CREST, NA.

64 'Representatives Fred Richmond and Richard Nolan, Discussions with Cuban President Fidel Castro', enclosed in Fred Richmond to Jimmy Carter (16 December 1977). White House Central File, BOX CO-20, JCL.

65 Memcon, Peter Tarnoff, Robert Pastor, Fidel Castro (Havana, 3–4 December 1978). Vertical File: Cuba, JCL. On 15 May 1964, the United States banned the export of medicines to Cuba.

66 Robert McFarlane, *Special Trust* (New York: Cadell & Davies, 1994), pp. 177–8.

67 'Remarks at the Annual Conference of the American Bar Association' (8 July 1985). Available at: www.presidency.ucsb.edu/ws/print.php?pid=388 54

68 *The New York Times* (26 January 1986), p. 10.

69 *The New York Times* (18 August 1985), p. 1.

70 Fidel Castro's 26 July 1989 speech, *Granma* (Havana, 28 July 1989), pp. 3–5.

71 Memorandum for Lt. Colonel B. W. Tarwater.

USAF, J-5, OJCS, NSF, BOX 61A, John F. Kennedy Library, Boston.

72 'Narrative of the Anti-Castro Cuban Operation Zapata' (13 June 1961), enclosed in Maxwell Taylor to President Kennedy, ibid.

73 CIA, Office of Current Intelligence, 'Weekly Cuban Summary' (31 March 1965). NSFCF, LBJL.

74 Quoted in Henry Ryan, *The Fall of Che Guevara: A Story of Soldiers, Spies, and Diplomats* (New York: Oxford University Press, 1998), p. 132.

75 *The Ethiopian Herald* (Addis Ababa, 19 December 2007), p. 1.

76 Thenjiwe Mtintso speech (Havana, 2 December 2005). Courtesy of Thenjiwe Mtintso.

77 General Ulises Rosales del Toro, Chief of the General Staff of the Cuban Armed Forces, to Army General Valentin Varennikov (5 September 1984). CIFAR.

78 Interview with Chester Crocker, Washington DC (18 May 2009).

79 'Aus der Aussprache mit Genossem Fidel Castro am 14. November 1968 während des Mittagessens im Gürtel von Havanna' [From the Discussion with Comrade Fidel Castro on 14

November 1968 during Lunch in the Outskirts of Havana]. DY30 IVA 2/20/205, SAPMO.

80 Memcon, Fidel Castro, José Eduardo dos Santos (Luanda, September 1986). CIFAR.

81 Jon David Glassman, 'Oral History Interview', Association for Diplomatic Studies and Training, Washington DC (ADST).

82 'Geagte Kollega' (20 May 1981). Briewe van minister van Buitelandse Sake en Inligting, VOL. 2, DFA.

83 CIA, Directorate of Intelligence, 'Angola: Prospects for MPLA–UNITA Reconciliation' (February 1985). FOIA.

84 Edward Perkins to SecState (17 April 1987). FOIA.

85 Interview with Stephen Weissman, Washington DC (10 April 2005).

86 SecState to Amembassy Pretoria (5 December 1987). FOIA.

87 'Reunión de análisis de la situación de las tropas cubanas en la RPA, efectuada a partir de las 17:25 horas del 15.11.1987' [Meeting to Analyse the Situation of the Cuban troops in the PRA, conducted from 17:25 hours on 15.11.1987]. CIFAR.

88 Mikhail Gorbachev to Fidel Castro (5 December 1987). CIFAR.

89 Memcon, Fidel Castro, Joe Slovo (Havana, 29 September 1988). CIFAR.

90 Jan Breytenbach, *Buffalo Soldiers: The Story of South Africa's 32 Battalion 1975–1993* (Alberton: Galago, 2002), p. 308; US Joint Chiefs of Staff (15 April 1988). NSA.

91 Chester Crocker, *High Noon in Southern Africa: Making Peace in a Rough Neighborhood* (New York: W. W. Norton, 1992), p. 379.

92 US Deputy Assistant Secretary of State for Africa Charles Freeman, 'Oral History Interview'. ADST.

93 US Joint Chiefs of Staff (28 July 1988). NSA.

94 Memcon, Jorge Risquet, Chester Crocker (Cairo, 26 June 1988). ACC.

95 Amembassy Brazzaville to SecState (25 August 1988). NSA.

96 Mike Malone to A. Jacquet, enclosed in Jacquet to Pik Botha (20 July 1988). SWA/Angola, VOL. 2, DFA.

97 SADF, 'Samevatting van notas mbt SAW-operasies in Suid-Angola' [Summary of Notes about

SADF Operations in Southern Angola] (23 August 1988). H SAW, GR. 4, BOX 160, Department of Defence, Documentation Centre, Pretoria.

98 Nelson Mandela speech, *Granma* (Havana, 27 July 1991), p. 3.

99 CIA, 'Latin America Review Supplement' (3 August 1978). RAC, JCL.

100 Kenneth Skoug, in *The New York Times* (9 June 1985), p. 9.

101 'Cuban Objectives in Africa', enclosed in Vest to Hibbert (11 August 1977). FCO 99/22, Public Record Office, Kew, Surrey.

102 Raúl Castro, 'Septima Reunión con Neto' [Seventh Meeting with Neto] (26 May 1976). ACC.

103 Memcon, Fidel Castro, José Eduardo dos Santos (Havana, 19 March 1984). CIFAR.

104 CIA, 'Latin America Review Supplement' (3 August 1978). RAC, JCL.

105 Lourdes Franco Codinach to her mother, Benguela (27 July 1988). Havana: private collection.

106 Interview with Berhanu Dibaba, Havana (15 December 2006).

107 Richard Cohen, 'Mandela: A Mistake in Cuba', *The Washington Post* (30 July 1991), p. 15; Mandela speech, *Granma*.

108 Coltman, *The Real Fidel Castro*, p. 289.

109 Nelson Mandela, Address to Cuba Solidarity Conference, Johannesburg (6–8 October 1995). Available at: http://www.freedompark.co.za

Suggested Reading

Historians of Cuban foreign policy after 1959 are crippled by the fact that the Cuban archives are closed. Unless otherwise noted, none of the studies listed below uses Cuban documents.

The best biography of Fidel Castro, by far, is Tad Szulc's *Fidel: A Critical Portrait* (New York: William Morrow, 1986). Two recent works should be noted: Leycester Coltman's *The Real Fidel Castro* (New Haven: Yale University Press, 2003) combines insight with factual error; and Ignacio Ramonet's *Cien Horas con Fidel* [One Hundred Hours with Fidel] (3rd rev. edn, Havana: Officina de Publicaciones del Consejo de Estado, 2006) is a very lengthy interview with Fidel Castro [English edn: *Fidel Castro: My Life—A Spoken Biography* (London: Allen Lane, 2007)].

Three accounts of foreign policy written by Cuban protagonists are particularly valuable: Ernesto Che Guevara's *Pasajes de la guerra revolucionaria: Congo* (Aleyda March, ed.) (Barcelona: Editorial Sudam, 1999)—written for Fidel Castro, it is Guevara's account of the Cuban column he led in eastern Zaire in 1965 [English edn: *The African Dream: The Diaries of the Revolutionary War in Congo* (London: Harvill, 2000)]; Jorge Risquet Valdés' *El segundo frente del Che en el Congo. Historia del batallón Patricio Lumumba* [Che's Second Front in the Congo: A History of the Patrice Lumumba Batallion] (2nd rev. edn, Havana: Casa Editora Abril, 2006) is a well-documented and compelling account of the activities of the Cuban column that Risquet led in the former French Congo in 1965–66; José Gómez Abad's *Como el Che burló a la CIA* [How Che Mocked the CIA] (Spain: Rústica, 2007), written by a Cuban intelligence officer, is the only study of Cuban support for armed struggle in Latin America that is based on a large number of Cuban intelligence documents.

The best history of Castro's Cuba is Richard Gott's *Cuba: A New History* (New Haven: Yale University Press, 2004). Alexandr Fursenko and Timothy Naftali's '*One Hell of a Gamble*': *Khrushchev, Castro and Kennedy, 1958–1964* (New York: W. W. Norton, 1997) is the only study of Cuban–Soviet relations that relies on an important number of Soviet documents; unfortunately, it is marred by serious

factual mistakes about the Cuban revolutionary process.
See also Jacques Lévesque, *L'URSS et la révolution cubaine*
[The USSR and the Cuban Revolution] (Montreal: Presses
de la Fondation nationale des sciences politiques, 1976) and
the memoirs of two Soviet ambassadors in Cuba: V. I.
Vorotnikov, *Havana–Moskva: pamiatnie godu* [Havana–
Moscow: Memorable Years] (Moscow: S. Yu. Sajarova, G.
G. Fiedorov, 2001); and Alexandr Kapto, *Na perekrestkakh
zhizni: politicheskie memuary* [On the Crossroads of Life:
Political Memoirs] (Moscow: Sotsial 'no-politicheskii
zhurnal', 1996).

The best studies of US–Cuban relations are Wayne
Smith, *The Closest of Enemies: A Personal and Diplomatic
Account of U.S.–Cuban Relations since 1957* (New York: W. W.
Norton, 1987), which focuses on the Carter years; and Lars
Schoultz, *That Infernal Little Cuban Republic: The United States
and the Cuban Revolution* (Chapel Hill: The University of
North Carolina Press, 2009). Also useful are Morris Mor-
ley, *Imperial State and Revolution: The United States and Cuba,
1952–1986* (Cambridge: Cambridge University Press,
1987); and Don Bohning, *The Castro Obsession: U.S. Covert
Operations against Cuba 1959–1965* (Dulles, VA: Potomac
Books, 2005). Henry Ryan's *The Fall of Che Guevara: A Story
of Soldiers, Spies, and Diplomats* (New York: Oxford University Press, 1998) is the best study of the US response to the
guerrilla insurgency in Bolivia led by Che Guevara. The

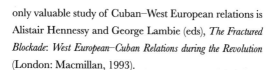

only valuable study of Cuban–West European relations is
Alistair Hennessy and George Lambie (eds), *The Fractured
Blockade: West European–Cuban Relations during the Revolution*
(London: Macmillan, 1993).

Boris Goldenberg's *Kommunismus in Lateinamerika*
[Communism in Latin America] (Stuttgart: Kohlhammer,
1971) is a superb analysis of the impact of the Cuban revolution on the Communist movement in Latin America in
the 1960s. Richard Gott's *Rural Guerrillas in Latin America*
(Harmondsworth: Penguin, 1973) is the best book on
armed struggle in Latin America in the 1960s. Régis
Debray's *A Critique of Arms*, 2 VOLS (Paris: Editions de Seuil,
1974), covers armed struggle in Latin America in the 1960s
and early 1970s and is based on the author's privileged ac-
cess to several guerrilla leaders and to Cuban officials [Eng-
lish edn: *A Critique of Arms* (New York: Penguin, 1977)]. Also
valuable is Daniel James (ed.), *The Complete Bolivian Diaries of
Ché Guevara and Other Captured Documents* (London: George
Allen and Unwin, 1968). Che Guevara's Bolivian diary,
however, is far less informative than his account of the operation in Zaire.

Since 1994, I have been able to conduct research in
the closed Cuban archives. For the results, see especially my
'Cuba and the Cold War, 1959–1980', in Melvyn Leffler
and Odd Arne Westad (eds), *The Cambridge History of the Cold
War* (Cambridge: Cambridge University Press, 2009), VOL.

2, pp. 327–48; 'Moscow's Proxy? Cuba and Africa 1975–88', *Journal of Cold War Studies* (Fall 2006): 98–146; *Conflicting Missions: Havana, Washington, and Africa, 1959–1976* (Chapel Hill: The University of North Carolina Press, 2002); 'Truth or Credibility: Castro, Carter, and the Invasions of Shaba', *International History Review* (February 1996): 70–103.

Three additional works, though not focusing on Cuba, shed light on Cuba's foreign policy: F. J. du Toit Spies, *Operasie Savannah. Angola 1975–1976* [Operation Savannah. Angola 1975–1976] (Pretoria: S. A. Weermag, 1989); Sophia du Preez, *Avontuur in Angola. Die verhaal van Suid-Afrika se soldate in Angola 1975–1976* [Adventure in Angola: The Story of South Africa's Soldiers in Angola 1975–1976] (Pretoria: J. L. Van Schaik, 1989); Nancy Mitchell, 'Race and Realpolitik: Jimmy Carter and Africa' (forthcoming, 2010). Spies and du Preez offer the only two studies of the South African operation in Angola in 1975–76 that are based on South African documents. Mitchell combines an unprecedented array of sources with a sophisticated analysis to offer what is by far the best study of Carter's policy in Africa. See also her 'The Cold War and Jimmy Carter', in Melvyn Leffler and Odd Arne Westad (eds), *The Cambridge History of the Cold War* (Cambridge: Cambridge University Press, 2009), VOL. 3, pp. 66–88.

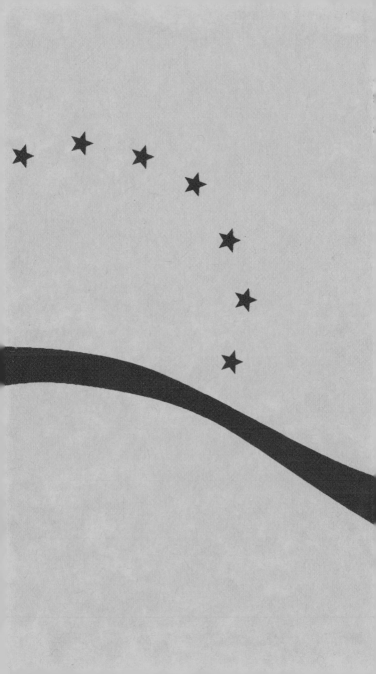